For Cameron and Daina,

Without whom I would never have considered the reality that we all need to keep our mental health in check, that sometimes we need to be reminded just how amazing we are with or without validation and that the strength lies within each of us to achieve goals, remain focused and be present in all things in our lives.

INDEX Chapters

The Sugar Honey Ice Tea Teenagers need to know

By

Melody de Robillard

Prologue

So, you're a Teenager. Congratulations! And WELCOME to the most incredible, crazy, great, confusing, exciting, trying, wonderful, awesome, stupid, fun, innocent, and hopefully happy time of your life.

You have the most dynamic JOB in the world right now, and with now being the only time you own forever, savour every moment. Live it to the fullest and learn, learn, learn.

This sounds nuts to a teenager, right? WRONG, young person of the planet! YOU, at your very core are a living, breathing, AMA-ZING, information-guzzling machine, soaking up every little bit of YouTube, news, Twitter, Facebook, Netflix, Instagram, classroom, playground news and internet information you see and hear. And all of this without even trying much.

You are processing all this information at a mile a minute and either spitting it out as fact or disposing of it as cap in mere milliseconds, and that, my dear, is the reason this book started to take shape.

With the internet and social media being your classroom for a lot of your guidance, the world is spinning at such incredible speeds that holding onto the important stuff in your developing mind has become harder and harder to decipher and remember. What with all the orals, schoolwork, Mom's and Dad's instructions "bleggh!", never mind maths and spelling, etc., how are you ever going to master the spirit of self, grit, and determination?

You, my amazing superstar, have this book filled with all the information you need on how to develop these skills, and if you practice these life lessons, you will understand yourself better and perhaps, your meaning and purpose for this life and prosper.

Read, practice, and use these chapters. Play them like you would a game and practice the art of being the perfect version of yourself.

GO ON—BE AMAZING!!

CHAPTER 1

Be the Colander

Firstly, some of you may not know what a colander is. It is essentially a kitchen tool used in cooking that helps the chef filter the good stuff away from the bad stuff.

Have you ever seen the chef in your life (Mom, Dad, Sister, Brother, Aunty, etc., etc.) take a boiling pot of rice or spaghetti and pour it into a metal container filled with holes? All that delicious goodness stays behind in the colander while the gunky, messy water just runs away through the holes down the drain.

This, my hero of this book, is what you need to do with the colander of your mind. Filter out all the bad arguments, comments, and times, and let them pour away through the holes while you hold onto all that good "yummy" goodness: feelings, words, and inspiration that fill you with joy.

By practicing being the colander, and not allowing any negativity to stay with you but be filtered away instead, you will become a master at recognising your own worth, realising every day just how special you are and making this work for your daily life.

Exercise

SECTION 1. Write down a moment here where you had an argument with someone, when someone was negative toward you, or what someone said negatively about you.

Write down all the words that hurt you that you can still remember!

HOLES
____

____

____

____

____

SECTION 2. Write down all the moments where you have been told how great you are, how loved you are, basically, everything you can remember. Even random comments, e.g.: your hair looks good, you have a beautiful smile or eyes, etc., will work here.

HOLD
____

____

____

____

____

READ ALL THE WORDS YOU HAVE WRITTEN IN BOTH SECTIONS
AGAIN.

Now, read this whole passage and then close your eyes and pour all those words into your colander—the whole steaming, bubbling, boiling lot of them—and watch the bad words filter out through the holes like gunky water being poured away. These words make me laugh because they are so weak, they can't stay behind. They can't hold onto the strong, good words, and they are so small they just slip right through the holes. Then, you can see what is left behind in your colander, you brilliant little warrior.

 ALL your wonderful yummy, delicious words are there.

These are the words you keep and consume daily. Whenever you need to, you can practice being the colander.

CHAPTER 2

Self-Doubt – Is Not Your FRIEND

Self-doubt is doubting YOU can do something, learn something, or play something and ultimately talking yourself down. When we hear ourselves and tell ourselves that we are not capable of doing something, what happens?

That's right, we fail, or we do poorly.

There are a few ways to work on self-doubt. Firstly, be prepared. I've heard this saying a lot in my life, so you may as well start now: If you FAIL TO PLAN, YOU PLAN TO FAIL! Another good one is "success loves preparation". And that means that if you do not prepare your day, your work schedule, your study schedule, or your practice schedule for sport, exercise, etc., chances are you are not going to do as well as you CAN do.

The first step is always just to plan and be prepared. Prepared is organised, and organised is prepared.

And sometimes, even then, we still have self-doubt! I have an example of a wonderful human being about the same age as you are reading this right now. He was in the middle of an important first round tennis match. he had won his first game and was on a high, feeling good, feeling prepared, and set to win. Please keep in mind that in junior tennis, there are a minimum of six games in each set and a minimum of two sets in a match, but he was still feeling good. He had won the first game, and so he should.

He was extremely well prepared and had a rigorous tennis schedule that ensured he was planning and had prepared to win. Halfway through the first set (so they were three games in), he found himself on the back foot. The other player had fought back and won two games, so now he had one game, and the other player had two. How he explained it to me was that it started small with one question in his mind, and then it just became bigger and bigger. "I wonder what people are thinking of my game", "I'm not good at tennis". "I don't even know why I am playing". "I can't serve the ball". "I can't even get the ball over the net". He sunk into despair and anxiety, and he lost his match in a flurry of self-doubt.

Self-doubt did that, people. NOTHING ELSE. He had the tools, skills, preparedness, and planning. He may still have lost, but he also may have fought back and won. He will never know because he allowed his self-doubt to take over and control his mind and the entire match, and in the end, self-doubt WON.

Exercise

Section 1 - Write down all the words you tell yourself when you are feeling self-doubt about something.

____

____

____

____

____

____

Section 2 – Write down all the words you would encourage your best friend with if they told you they were feeling this way about themselves.

____

____

____

____

____

____

THIS IS THE FUN STUFF—Write down your BEST FRIEND for LIFE's name (one name only). P.S. this can also be your mom, dad, sister, or brother.

____

____

Turn the Page!!!

SURPRISE!

YOUR BEST FRIEND FOR LIFE IS YOU.

Go back and read what you told yourself in section two because those are YOUR words that YOU would tell your Best Friend. Therefore, those are the words/phrases you need to use on yourself. YOU are your own best friend, and when you have self-doubt, say to yourself: 'What would I tell my best friend right now'? And tell yourself exactly what you need to hear to do better, be more confident, and be the best version of yourself. Eliminate any chance of Self-doubt. BE PREPARED. Plan and be organised then choose your best friend's advice first every time.

CHAPTER 3

Post-It

So far, you have learnt two incredible ways to feed your mind with positivity which will allow you to be the person you were and are destined to be. Whenever you need to, just sit down, re-read, and rework these past two chapters, and eventually, they will become part of your routine mental workout (yup). Just like you work out your body, so too must you work out your mind.

However, until you get there, you will need to Post-it. I say Post-it because adults call it 'affirmations', and I forget that word sometimes. So instead, let's just Post-it. Get a Post-it pad from your local stationer. A fabulous colourful one is best. If you can't get a Post-it pad, get colourful pens or crayons and write in different colours. If you can't do this, don't worry about that either. Just write it down and Post-it up.

Sit down in front of your mirror with a pen and start to write some messages about yourself that you need to be reminded of.

Remember, these are personal reminders for yourself, so just keep it simple for now. Your Post-it's are your truths about yourself, and they should make you feel good when you see them. They are not notes or words from someone else. These are notes to you from you. When you start needing more in-depth ones at a later stage, just pull out your Post-it pad again and rewrite your Post-its.

Some examples below:

I AM CAPABLE

I AM WORTHY

I LOVE MYSELF

I AM THE BEST TENNIS PLAYER

I AM THE BEST SPORTSPERSON

I AM KIND

I BELIEVE IN MY ABILITY

I HAVE THE ABILITY TO LEARN AND BE TAUGHT

I AM BEAUTIFUL

I AM PERFECT

As you write one, find the appropriate place to stick your Post-it. On the inside of your cupboard, on the back of your bedroom door, on your bedroom wall, in random places on your bathroom mirror, or on your bedroom mirror. Put them wherever you are going to see them every day and be reminded of all the special, wonderful things you are.

Every day, walk around your space paying special attention to each Post-it and say them to yourself three times, for example, "I believe in my ability", "I believe in my ability", "I believe in my ability". Then, close your eyes for the last one to soak it all in and move onto the next. Once each Post-it is complete, you should have your final one on a mirror. This one is the SECRET TO LIFE, young people. Look yourself dead in the eyes and say three times, "I LOVE YOU".

Loving yourself is the most fulfilling feeling in the world and will help you achieve your best every day because no matter what, you are LOVED. Drop the mic. BOOM! "MIND BLOWN, RIGHT"?

INTERLooDE

Yup, just like in the movies, there is a toilet break here because I know you have been reading this book and working it like a crazy person, so desperate to soak up these pearls of wisdom. Ok, so maybe you haven't, but just in case you have.

The interlude is here to remind you to practice each section. This is a reminder that without practice, there is no perfect. There is also no perfect. You doing you every day is what I mean by perfect. Just being you is perfect.

I'm hoping your mind is one giant colander by now, just overflowing with positivity.

CHAPTER 4

How Does Your Garden Grow?

Have you ever noticed how quickly a weed grows? If you have ever listened to a gardener or done some gardening yourself, you will know that you have to constantly be removing weeds from the garden because they pop up all the time. These are the unwanted plants in any garden that suffocate other plants and flowers, steal the light and generally, if left unwatched, overtake a garden and leave it looking uncared for and sad. Flowers, by comparison, take much longer to cultivate. They need lots of light, love, care, and special attention, which is why a lot of people tend to allow weeds to take over their garden—it's just easier!

Firstly, we are not talking about an actual garden here— SURPRISE☺

By now, you have figured out a theme in this book. Everything means something else.

So naturally, your garden is the garden of your mind.

So, my intrepid gardener, what have you planted in your garden, are they weeds or are they flowers?

Who are you surrounding yourself with? Ask yourself, how do these people make me feel? How do I behave around them? Am I confident and happy? Am I at ease? Do I feel uncared for and sad after I have spent time with them?

Write people's names in your life here:

____

____

____

____

Weeds vs. Flowers Comparison:

Write down each person in your life's name. and write down their influence on your life, negative or positive.

Name	Flowers	Weeds
E.g. –Friend Oliver	Makes me laugh, is kind to me, and tells me the truth	Nothing
E.g. – Friend Bruce	Sometimes makes me laugh	Makes me cry, normally shouts at me, and leaves me out of games or parties

Once you have completed this list, if there are more weeds than flowers to the person, then the person is a weed in your life, and they are not making your garden beautiful.

You now need to check on YOUR behaviour.

Write down your behaviour towards other friends, parents, or teachers after you have spent time with a weed or flower.

E.g., Bruce: After I spend time with Bruce, I am generally sad and depressed, and I don't want to talk to anyone. I want to be alone, and I feel small.

E.g., Oliver: After I spend time with Oliver, I am happy and cheerful, and I always have a good time with Mom in the car on the way home from school.

____

____

____

____

____

____

____

____

What have you noticed?

What you should have highlighted for yourself here is that the garden of your mind requires LIGHT, LOVE, CARE, AND SPECIAL ATTENTION.

Maybe it's easier to be with Bruce because he's always available (maybe now you know why). Get rid of the weed, my brave gardener. You can only achieve greater things by surrounding yourself with people that enrich your life and add to it, not take away from it.

CHAPTER 5

Tick Your Box

What does success look like to you? Write your idea of what a successful person looks like to you. Is it a sports star, a wealthy person, a superstar, a hero (like firemen/policemen)? These are just a few examples. You need to make it specific to your dreams and aspirations:

Remember, it is different for everybody. For most people though, it will probably be what you have written above, and if I'm correct in my thinking, you've written something like my example. Did you include someone with fame, riches, or fortune? Maybe. But maybe it's Mom or Dad too?

The important thing to note here is that success is not what is above in writing; these are the things you wish to aspire to in life, and that is great. You must have goals and dreams, dreams that you are working towards and wish to achieve.

Therefore, you need to be CLEAR in your thinking here. These are your long-term goals, dreams, and aspirations that you want to achieve in life when you are older.

Start smaller. Start with something that you want to achieve this semester, term, or quarter. Sometimes even starting with this week is easier.

Goals and Dreams:

Write yours here: When you can see them, you can achieve them!

E.g.: Pass a math test, get a D, C or B in Science, make the A team (in your chosen sport) learn to ride a bike, learn to surf or learn to cook.

____

____

____

____

____

____

____

Include some personal goals and aspirations.

Write yours here: When you can see them, you can achieve them!

E.g.: Be a better listener, be more helpful around the house, do my chores without my parent or caregiver asking, or grow my hair out

____

____

____

____

____

____

____

____

Success is every day:

Success is personal. It is not what everyone else says it is. It is you ticking your boxes. You choose what you want your success to be.

Come back to your list at the end of the week, semester, quarter, term, or year and tick your boxes. Even ticking one box is a success. Next week, semester, quarter, term, or year you will tick more and more until you are ticking all your boxes all the time. SUCCESS!

CHAPTER 6

Grit

Grit, what is it, where does it come from, and how do you get it?

Have you ever seen a gardener's hands? Hahaha, no, we are not gardening again. Well, not really. Normally when a gardener has been messing in the dirt, there are small particles of sand under their nails, also known as grit. This is an expression of how hard they have worked in the garden because you can see the grit under their nails.

GRIT is also an expression of someone with perseverance, courage, passion and strength of character.

Someone with GRIT, sets goals, works towards them, and never gives up.

An example of someone with true GRIT is Greta Thunberg. She is an advocate for climate change and, from the age of fifteen, has been rallying against government and politicians to make change.

Someone else with true GRIT are the moms, dads and caregivers working hard at their jobs to keep food on the table for their families.

These are two quite different examples, and there are many others to list, but as long as you are working towards something of importance to you and being KIND with good intentions along the way, you are starting to form your own GRITTY nature, which will, in turn, become full-blown GRIT.

Be determined in the pursuit of your dreams, be consistent in your daily quest, young knights and maidens. The future is bright, and you can forge your path by staying true to yourself.

Look in your environment at the people you see every day, people who work hard, are kind, and helpful. Even if they don't have everything, they are putting in a full day's work and showing true GRIT.

They can be your teachers, your grocery store attendant, Mom or Dad?

Write your own examples here:

____

____

____

____

____

____

____

____

Use these examples to guide you in your behaviour and intentions in your own life; you will note that when you have set goals for your everyday success, GRIT will come naturally.

YOU ARE THE GRIT. BE THE GRIT!!

CHAPTER 7

Watch a Good Movie

Sorry, Guys and Gals, I've just tricked you here. Although having said that, a good movie that will inspire you is never a bad thing. Also, any movie that will whisk you away to a place of euphoria (look it up 😊) is great.

This is a section on VISUALISATION. Yup, you are going to learn to VISUALISE (or watch a good movie, the best movie really) your life before it happens.

When all is quiet, and you are in bed at night, that is normally the best time to peacefully VISUALISE the coming day's events for yourself.

Start first by relaxing your body one part at a time, closing your eyes, and relaxing your head, shoulders, arms, chest, hips, legs, knees, and finally, feet. Once every part of your body feels relaxed, calm, and still, start your movie reel in your mind.

Start with a successful, happy wake up, a good breakfast, and everything going to plan, making your way to school, and being on time. Then, VISUALISE spending time at school and having great classes with teachers. Watch yourself enjoy your classes including the lessons you are not usually fond of. VISUALIZE all of them being good. Watch your movie take you to spending time with friends and having a fun time at break. VISUALISE all the way home again until bedtime.

After you VISUALISED a good day the night before, when you get home the next day, note here how your day was:

____

____

____

____

____

____

____

You may notice that in comparison to other days, that it was, in fact, an incredibly good day. Don't you find that amazing? You mentally prepared yourself for an awesome day, and it happened!! You Rock!

You do not have to do VISUALISATIONS daily. However, what they can do for you, is this: when you have a truly important event coming up in your life that you are either stressed, worried, or feel anxiety about, you can VISUALISE it going well.

Just like VISUALISING having a good day, you can VISUALISE a sports match and your role in the sports match (remember you must have put in the work with your GRIT and preparedness) or an exam you have studied for. Or perhaps you have a fear of public speaking, and once again, the teacher has set an oral which requires you to verbalise it in front of the class. VISUALISE your oral going well (Prepared is organised. practice, practice, practice your oral) and VISUALISE it frequently leading up to the event.

You will be amazed at how incredibly well it goes in comparison to previous orals.

I will be cheering for you all the way, you CHAMPION GRITTY HUMAN.

CHAPTER 8

Get Up,

Dress Up,

Show Up

GET UP, DRESS UP, and SHOW UP is the daily requirement, isn't it? We all have to do this anyway, right? Why on Earth is there a chapter dedicated to this? This is the simplest thing to do.

Well, you would think so. But, it is ABSOLUTLEY unbelievable how many people struggle with waking up in the morning, getting dressed, and showing up. And I don't just mean for school or for work. I mean for your OWN LIFE, man. Show up daily with a smile and a goal that will give you purpose in your day.

Show up for _______________________________ (put your name here)

YES! Your life requires you to GET UP, DRESS UP, and SHOW UP. This means to be present in every way possible.

A routine for your day is key here.

Develop healthy routines for GIDDY UPS –

1. Go to bed Early
2. Wake up on time (use an alarm clock if you can't do this alone)
3. Eat Breakfast
4. Continue from here ___________________________
5. ____
6. ____
7. ____
8. ____
9. ____

List as many routines as you need to get going in the morning. Remember, part of your routine is getting dressed and showing up. I've started it for you with wake up!

If you've already got a routine that is perfect, well done! You are ahead of the pack. Continue, don't stop. Keep showing up for your life.

If you are a new GIDDY UPPER, do not despair. You can start SHOWING UP for your life at any time. The important thing is just to start—the sooner, the better—and if you start now, you are ahead of ninety per cent of the planet, my majestic hero, because ninety per cent of the planet do not show up. So, get going now. ☺

YOU'VE GOT THIS!

CHAPTER 9

Map Out Your Day

It just seems fitting that we should follow the GIDDY UP chapter with time management. Yup, mapping out your day is all about time management, people.

When you become successful at your routine, you will master your time management and be able to complete tasks and allocate time to all the important stuff in your day and life.

Not all time management is boring, by the way. It is for you to schedule time for friends, games, food, downtime, sleep, family, exercise/sport, crafts, etc., or whatever is good for your soul, the stuff that makes you whole.

Your school day is already scheduled for you; it is already time managed, with bells and expectations and deadlines for projects, orals, and dates for exams. So that is an excellent example of what a schedule looks like; however, how do you manage one for yourself? I guess you would have to fit homework in there somewhere and some studying, but this is such a small portion of your time and energy if you look at the bigger picture.

This is especially true if you are practicing GIDDY UPPING already. You are present all the time in class. This means that you can really get through your studies with a clear, focused mind quickly and efficiently and stick to your schedule as mapped out by you.

Time Management—Schedule

E.g.: A day in the life of our gardener 😊

	Monday	Tuesday	Wednesday	Thursday	Friday
6am	GIDDY UP & Post-It routine				
7am	Bus to work				
8am	Start work				
2:30pm	Finish work				
2:45pm	Bus home				
3:00pm	Plant new seeds for new veggies to grow, trim, and pull out the weeds, and turn the soil.				
4:00pm	Chill time: Call a friend, read a book, exercise, or play Fortnight				

4:45pm	Pick veggies for dinner				
5pm	Cup of tea, shower and scrub the grit from my fingers				
5:30pm	Start dinner				
6pm	Dinner with the family, Family time till 7				
7pm	Read a book				
7:30pm	VISUALISE the day ahead				
8pm	SLEEP				

Now fill in the rest of the week with your schedule— allocating time to all the important tasks in your life. You will find you have more than enough time for homework and plenty of time for friends, family, and chill time once you can view it here.

CHAPTER 10

Chemicals

This, my dear teenage traveller, is an important chapter. LISTEN UP!

HAPPINESS CHEMICALS? YES!

Did you know there used to be bubble gum and still is in South Africa called a Chappie. Chappies developed a wrapper that you can read random general knowledge about the world on. Well, this is a "Did you know?" chapter.

Did you know that we humans have HAPPINESS CHEMICALS that course through our veins, and we can tap into them (turn on the tap) at any time we like? Here they are, and this is what they can do for you.

Dopamine sounds dope, right?

DOPAMINE—The reward chemical

1. Eating Food

Your body immediately responds to eating food. In fact, have you ever noticed how happy you feel as soon as you know you can sit down to eat when you're hungry?

Pay attention to how you feel after you've eaten. Are you feeling relieved, happy, content, satisfied, and fulfilled?

Write down foods that make you feel good and remember to include healthy foods. This includes meals shared with family and friends.

Food and meals that make me feel good:

____

____

____

Achieving a Goal

Those simple success goals you set for yourself earlier will help you get some Dopamine and feel a sense of achievement which in turn makes you brim with pride.

Keep your list of successes updated:

2. Getting Enough Sleep

Yup, you will be ready to GIDDY UP and get on with your day like a recharged battery with enough sleep and a whole lot of Dopamine coursing through your body.

Set yourself a bedtime limit. You are not missing out on anything good if you do sleep, but you are missing out on some Dope Dopamine if you don't!

3. Having a Bath

Cleaning your body washes away the dirt and grime of the day and leaves you with a sense of newness and renewed sense of energy.

Enjoy your bath/shower time. Smell your skin after a shower and notice that small smile that creeps onto your lips just because you smell good.

Who's Ox?

OXYTOCIN— The Love Hormone

1. Socialising

Spending time with quality people and friends that are flowers in the garden of your mind and life will fill you with both Oxytocin and positivity.

Keeping the flower friends watered will flow over into your life, and when you need some love, you will find it in these friendships

2. Physical Touch

A hug from Mom or Dad or a high five from a friend will give you a grounded feeling and a sense of belonging and comfort.

When you are feeling low, note how a good ol' hug from a loved one can suddenly lift your spirits and make you feel good. Don't be afraid to ask for one when you need it. You need Oxytocin. Demand your shot!

3. Petting Animals

Playing with an animal, be it your neighbours, your own, or a friend's, will give you the feel-good feeling that only an animal can give you.

Animals have long since been proven to be a wonderful source of security, love, and comfort, as well as a delicious provider of the chemical Oxytocin. Even watching animal videos on YouTube has become a past time that people have turned to in order to get their Oxytocin hit during an incredibly difficult day. Seek out an animal or watch a YouTube video of animals, and you'll start increasing your love hormone and feel better faster.

4. Helping Others

When we step out of ourselves and our comfort zones to help others, it fills us with a sense of being one with our surroundings and all of the other humans on Earth. You are then rewarded with a huge amount of love for your fellow man.

This naturally translates to your community as well. Find a cause that you are drawn to that fills you with pride when you are helping out, and support those in need.

List places in your community here that you would like to be a part of:

____

____

____

____

Now look out for opportunities to be a part of your community in the way's above.

Dada dee dada dum!

ENDORPHIN— The Pain Killer

1. Exercising

Did you know that if you sprain your ankle, the best medicine is to use it straight away? this in turn reduces the amount of pain by diminishing the days that you are incapacitated, and the same goes for any injury. Don't be in a rush or anything, but get exercising as soon as you can, will help you heal quicker. Also, exercising can help reduce sadness and depression as well as increase your energy levels.

The quicker we recover from any kind of painful experience, whether it be physical or emotional, the quicker we can move on with our day-to-day life. So, seek out the best course of action for your pain, whether it be to hug a friend, Mom, or Dad, go for long walks, and exercise the ailment. Find a solution and increase your energy levels.

2. Laughing

When we express laughter out loud, it releases ENDORPHINS that make us feel good all over. There used to be a hospital in the USA called The Silly Hospital that was run by Doctor Patch Adams and his fellow colleagues. Besides medicine, they used humour to improve the health of their patients. That's REMARKABLE!

It really works, people! Watch your favourite comedy, look up some jokes, tell the jokes to friends, and find humour in any situation. The sillier you can make it, the quicker you can overcome your embarrassment, sadness, or pain and laugh it off. We are all human. No one is perfect, but we are all perfectly ourselves.

3. Listening to Music – (uplifting music can increase your mood dramatically from down and sombre to happy and elated, keep a good selection at hand whenever you need a lift)

Go make a playlist now.

Find your favourite uplifting music. It does not and should not, in fact, be what anyone else likes. Sometimes it is, but that does not matter either. This is personal. This is all about you getting a kickstart of some ENDORPHINS into your day, moment, or time in your life when you need them most. Play the heck out of that playlist whenever you need it. You'll be on the road to feeling good soon.

Toes have nothing to do with this!

SEROTONIN— The mood stabilizer

1. This one is a toughie because too much, and you are in trouble, but too little, and you're depressed. So, to keep you stabilised is a daily work out for your senses. Keep in mind, young intrepid teenager, that you have quite a few tricks and tips in the previous chapters above to help you cope with some potentially mood displacing moments. Meditating

Taking time out of your day to be still and quiet is essential to keeping a healthy mind.

Try to set time aside, whether it be first thing in the morning, last thing at night, or even in the middle of day, it really does not matter. Spend five minutes with yourself daily, thinking of nothing and sitting in a relaxed pose with no distractions. This is meditating. It's one of the most difficult things to do, and yet it seems so easy. If your mind starts to wander and you think of school, friends, chores, etc., gently remind yourself to go back to nothing. Think of nothing for five minutes a day and you can increase this time when you are ready. But start with five minutes.

2. Sun Exposure

Walking in the great outdoors for a minimum of fifteen minutes a day will help to increase your SEROTONIN levels and keep your mood in a good place.

Your lunch break is best had outdoors on a bench— even if you only do one of your breaks a day outdoors, try for at least one.

3. Walk in Nature

Get back to nature and the many health benefits of being out in the wild.

Even if you don't have a place to walk in nature, take a walk in the park. This is nature. Take your shoes off and feel the grass under your feet. It's called grounding, and grounding yourself has huge benefits like feeling calm and relaxed and at one with your universe and planet.

4. Deep Breathing

Ever heard someone say take a breath? That's exactly what you need to do here. Count to ten at medium pace and breathe in. Then, breathe out to the count of eight at medium pace. Do this four times.

This helps relieve anxiety and clear your mind – you can also do this to go to sleep if that is something you struggle with.

ON A SERIOUS NOTE:

If you ever find yourself feeling sad and miserable every day, if you can't get out of bed or you don't want to or that everything you look at is in shades of grey— speak to a counsellor, a teacher, or your parents and seek help. There is only so much these natural remedies can do for your daily mood enhancement. You may need more sincere conversations or assistance to help you get back on the right track. NEVER ever feel uncomfortable with telling someone you need help. This is a sign of the fighting spirit inside of you to survive and be well with your fellow man the world around you and yourself.

CHAPTER 11

Social Media

#justsaying SOCIAL MEDIA is not social at all.

Having face to face conversations with your friends and family is being social.

Having said that, some people are less comfortable being face to face with people, and that is how social media was born.

What has happened though, is that the social creatures who love face to face contact with others and love attention have turned to social media to increase their social presence, while some have become influencers and made real jobs and money out of the social media scene. You can too if this is what interests you.

My point behind this chapter is not that it is good or bad or otherwise. Be very, very careful what you buy into on social media. Not everything you see and read is real, bullying happens on social media too, and sometimes it is worse than what happens in the real world. It's easier to hide behind a computer or cell phone screen and be mean to others without having the same consequences. The social media police, if I can call them that, are starting to and have been for some time starting to take this more seriously and are cracking down on social crime, so never put anything up or post anything that is cruel, mean, demeaning, offensive. Don't say anything if it's not something you would easily say or do in front of Mom, Dad, friends, teachers and peers because then, sweet peas, you know it's wrong!

Be careful of what is on offer on social media. There are predators out there that are waiting to prey on young, beautiful minds, and you are their perfect prey. Don't be the cute buck with big eyes stuck behind headlights. Choose your friends, know your friends, and don't accept anybody you don't know. Popularity is not what you are going for on social media. You want real friends that can help increase your DOPAMINE, for heck's sake. Come on now, this thumbs up 'like' on a computer screen is hardly a DOPAMINE kick worth feeling good about.

GO hug a puppy, trust me. It is ten times more DOPE.

CHAPTER 12

You Are Perfect

The poem below is a reminder that no matter what is going on in your life, you can change the way you view the situation. You are perfectly you and are gaining new perspectives every day. Keep at it, young knights and maiden's, the world is truly your oyster.

This poem is the original work of the Poet - Abdullah Shoaib.

<u>Pretty Ugly – by Abdullah Shoaib</u>

I'm very ugly

So don't try to convince me that

I am a very beautiful person

Because at the end of the day

I hate myself in every single way

And I'm not going to lie to myself by saying

There is beauty inside of me that matters

So rest assured I will remind myself

That I am worthless, terrible person

And nothing you say will make me believe

I still deserve love

Because no matter what

I am not good enough to be loved

And I am in no position to believe that

Beauty does exist within me

Because whenever I look in the mirror I always think

Am I as ugly as people say?

(Now READ From the bottom up) ---

Notes

Notes

Notes